TEAM SPIRIT
SMART BOOKS FOR YOUNG FANS

THE DALLAS MAVERICKS

BY
MARK STEWART

NORWOOD HOUSE PRESS

Norwood House Press
2544 Clinton Street
Buffalo, NY 14224

Photos courtesy of: Getty Images (Cover, 4, 14, 29, 35 bottom), Associated Press (6, 8, 9, 10, 12, 18, 19, 22, 23, 24, 25, 26, 27, 30, 33, 35 top, 37, 38, 39, 41, 42 both, 43 bottom, 45), Beckett Publications (7), Author's Collection (11, 21, 34, 36, 43 top), Star Co. (15), Topps, Inc. (17), Dell Publishing (31).

The memorabilia, artifacts, and media images that are pictured in this book are presented for educational and informational purposes and come from the collection of the author.

Art Director: Lisa Miley
Series Design: Ron Jaffe
Project Management: Upper Case Editorial Services LLC
Special thanks to Topps, Inc.

Names: Stewart, Mark, 1960 July 7-.
Title: The Dallas Mavericks / Mark Stewart.
Description: Buffalo, NY : Norwood House Press, 2025. | Series: Team spirit | Includes glossary and index.
Identifiers: ISBN 978-1-6845-0078-9 (pbk.) | ISBN 978-1-6845-0079-6 (library bound) | ISBN 978-1-6845-0080-2 (ebook)
Subjects: LCSH: Dallas Mavericks (Basketball team)--Juvenile literature. | Dallas Mavericks (Basketball team)--History--Juvenile literature.
Classification: LCC GV885.52.D34 S84 2025 | DDC 796.323'64--dc23

378N—022324
Manufactured in the United States of America in North Mankato, Minnesota.

TABLE OF CONTENTS

ABOUT OUR GLOSSARY

In this book, there may be several words that you are reading for the first time. Some are sports words, some are new vocabulary words, and some are familiar words that are used in an unusual way. All of these words are defined on page 46. Throughout the book, sports words appear in **bold type**. Regular vocabulary words appear in *bold italic type*.

MAKING THE MAVERICKS

Athletes on teams with cool animal names try their best to live up to that creature's image. When a player makes the Dallas Mavericks, he sees *himself* as a maverick—a young horse that breaks away from the herd. When the Mavericks are playing well, opponents have a hard time trying to stop them.

The fans in Dallas are among the most loyal in basketball. Through all of the team's ups and downs, they have filled the arena and encouraged the players to do well. The "Mavs" have rewarded those fans by playing winning basketball.

This book tells the story of the Mavericks. They are not afraid to think "outside the box" and look for players in places other teams don't. The Mavs know there is no set way to win, and that basketball is not a one-size-fits-all sport.

Luka Doncic and Kyrie Irving enjoy an overtime victory in 2024 on the way to the NBA Finals. The two stars were born in Slovenia and Australia—nearly 10,000 miles apart. The Mavericks have had great luck finding players whose basketball journey began in faraway places.

BUILDING BLOCKS

When sports leagues decide to start a new team, they look for growing cities. Dallas, Texas, had fewer than 50,000 people in 1900. By 1980, the city was home to nearly a million people. That year, the Mavericks played their first game. Now the area around Dallas had grown to almost 2.5 million people.

The Mavs were not the first *professional* basketball team to call Dallas home. In 1967, the Chaparrals were one of the original teams in the **American Basketball Association (ABA)**, a rival league to the **National Basketball Association (NBA)**. The Chaparrals did not have many fans. They moved to San Antonio and became the Spurs. The Mavericks had much better luck in Dallas. The fans warmed up to them right away.

Dick Motta was the team's first head coach. His top players were Brad Davis, Tom LaGarde, and Jim Spanarkel. Dallas won only 15 games in 1980–81, but the following season, three talented young players joined the team: Mark Aguirre, Jay Vincent, and Rolando Blackman.

In 1983–84, the Mavs made it to the **playoffs** and defeated the Seattle SuperSonics (now the Oklahoma City Thunder) in their first series. Aguirre became an **All-Star** that season, and newcomer Sam Perkins was one of the NBA's best **rookies**. The Mavericks added more good players to their lineup, including Derek Harper, Roy Tarpley, James Donaldson, and Detlef Schrempf. In 1986–87, they finished first in the **Midwest Division**. One year later, Dallas advanced all the way to the finals of the **Western Conference**. It took seven games for the Los Angeles Lakers to defeat them.

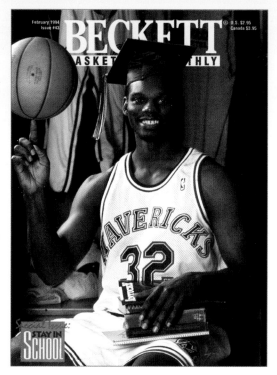

As the stars of the 1980s began to fade, the Mavericks found it difficult to replace them. The losses piled up in the early 1990s, but the fans continued to support the club. The bright side of this story was that the team's poor record meant it got high picks in the **draft**. The Mavs used their picks wisely and added Jim Jackson, Jamal Mashburn, and Jason Kidd to the team. They were known around the

LEFT: Brad Davis looks for an open teammate. He finished among the NBA leaders in assists six times.   **ABOVE**: Jamal Mashburn was just 21 when he posed for this magazine cover.

NBA as the "Three J's." Jackson could score from anywhere on the court. Mashburn was a dunking machine. Kidd was one of the best young guards in basketball. The Three J's played well, but a winning team needs more than three players. Most nights, Dallas ended up on the short end of the score.

Things began to change after Don Nelson was hired to coach the Mavericks. He built a new team around three different stars: Steve Nash, Michael Finley, and Dirk Nowitzki. Nelson was one of the first NBA coaches to blend the talents of players from different countries. The Mavericks had stars from Europe, South America, Africa, and Asia in their lineup. In just a few seasons, Dallas developed into one of the NBA's best teams.

During the 1999–2000 season, Mark Cuban bought the Mavericks. Cuban ran a computer *software* company, but his first love was basketball. He promised the fans of Dallas that he would do everything he could to bring them their first championship.

Cuban decided to build around Nowitzki, who was an unusual

LEFT: Jason Kidd scores against the Clippers. He was named NBA Rookie of the Year in 1995.   **ABOVE**: Don Nelson and Mark Cuban watch the Mavericks practice.

player. Nowitzki stood seven feet tall, but he was unlike other big men in the NBA. As a boy in Germany, he had learned basketball as a guard. When he grew, his coaches moved him to forward. Eventually, he became a center, but he never lost the skills he developed playing those other positions. The team tried many different combinations of players around Nowitzki, but finding a championship formula wasn't easy.

In 2004, Avery Johnson was picked to coach the Mavs. He let Nowitzki run the offense. This seemed like a strange choice for a coach who had once been a point guard. However, it turned out to be a *stroke of genius*. Johnson combined the talents of Josh Howard, Jerry Stackhouse, Jason Terry, Devin Harris, and Erick Dampier to create a team that was very hard to match up against.

In 2005–06, the Mavericks reached the **NBA Finals** for the first time. They faced the Miami Heat and won the first two games of the series. The next four games were all close, but the Heat found a way to win each one and the Mavs went home empty handed.

Nowitzki was super-focused on winning a championship after that. He seemed to get better each year. But Dallas fans worried that age and injuries might soon catch up with their beloved star.

In 2008–09, Cuban hired Rick Carlisle to coach the Mavs. Three years later, Dallas made it back to the NBA Finals. Jason Kidd returned to the club, and he and Nowitzki led the Mavericks to their first championship. They did so with help from *veterans* Shawn Marion, Tyson Chandler, Peja Stojakovic, Brendan Haywood, and J.J. Barea.

Nowitzki retired in 2019, leaving the Mavericks to wonder where they would find their next great player. It turned out there was no need for concern because that player was already on the team. Another young European star, Luka Doncic, played his first season beside Nowitzki and led the team in scoring at the age of 20.

Doncic was a 6' 7" guard who could take over games single-handedly. He made one *astonishing* play after another, bringing NBA fans leaping out of their seats. In 2022, Jason Kidd became the team's coach. Kidd was known for his *unselfish* teamwork as a player. That combination of talent and leadership won a championship for Dallas in 2011 and nearly won another in 2024. Doncic, Kyrie Irving, and Dereck Lively II helped the team return to the NBA Finals, but the Mavs fell to the powerhouse Boston Celtics.

LEFT: Dirk Nowitzki averaged more than 20 points a game 12 years in a row for Dallas. **ABOVE**: Luka Doncic's game-changing ability made his autograph is one of the hottest in all of sports.

GAME DAY

In the 1980s and 1990s, the Mavericks played in Reunion Arena. The building was named after La Réunion, a community near Dallas in the mid-1800s. It promoted the sharing of labor and equality between men and women.

Since 2001, the Mavericks have played their home games in an arena they share with the Dallas Stars hockey team. The arena has three-sided shot clocks, so everyone in the crowd knows how much time is left to shoot. Owner Mark Cuban ordered these clocks when a fan pointed out that not everyone could see the old single-sided ones at either end of the court.

BY THE NUMBERS

- The Mavs' arena has 19,200 seats for basketball, but it can hold more than 21,000 for playoff games.

- The arena cost $420 million to build.

- As of the 2023–24 season, the Mavericks have retired four uniform numbers: 12 (Derek Harper), 15 (Brad Davis), 22 (Rolando Blackmon), and 41 (Dirk Nowitzki).

The Mavs' arena offers lots of great views of the court.

TEAM COLORS

The Mavericks' team colors include royal blue, navy blue, silver, white, and black. When the team started, its colors were bright blue and green. The Mavs still wear special uniforms with these old colors from time to time. They tried red and silver uniforms for a few games during 2003–04, but the fans liked their other colors better.

The team *logo* has also changed over the years. For a long time, it featured the letter *M* inside a basketball that was topped by a cowboy hat. In 2001, Dallas switched to a stylish horse set against a blue basketball.

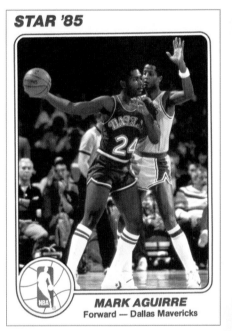

STAR '85

MARK AGUIRRE
Forward — Dallas Mavericks

LEFT: Dereck Lively II battles LeBron James for a rebound wearing the team's navy blue home uniform. **ABOVE**: This trading card shows Mark Aguirre in the Mavs' green 1980s road uniform.

15

LAST TEAM STANDING

The Mavericks were an NBA "expansion" team, which means they joined the league when it expanded from 22 teams to 23. Expansion teams are allowed to pick players from the other clubs, but the stars on those clubs are *off-limits*. That is why it can take many years for a team like the Mavericks to build a winner. Even so, it took the Mavs 30 years before they were the last team standing when the buzzer sounded at the end of the 2011 NBA Finals.

The team got close to the title several times. In 1987–88 and again in 2002–03, the Mavs made it to the Western Conference Finals. Both times, they ran into stronger opponents and fell short of a trip to the championship round.

In 2005–06, Dallas put together an attacking team led by Dirk Nowitzki. He got plenty of help from Jason Terry, Josh Howard, and Jerry Stackhouse. The Mavericks *surged* through the playoffs and finally advanced to the NBA Finals, against the Miami Heat. Dallas won the first two games of the series, but then Dwyane Wade took over for the Heat. He put on one of the great **postseason** performances in NBA history and led Miami to victory, 4 games

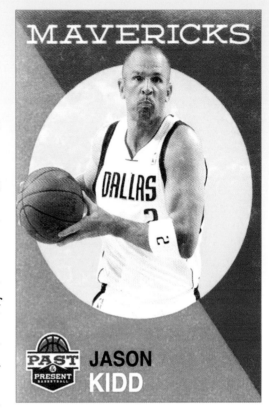

This 2011 "Past & Present" trading card celebrates Jason Kidd's triumphant return to Dallas.

to 2. Three of the Mavs' four losses in the series were narrow defeats.

The Mavericks learned valuable lessons from that experience. They began rebuilding their roster for playoff success. Dallas kept Nowitzki and Terry, and then surrounded them with a new group of veterans. Jason Kidd, a star for Dallas in the 1990s, returned to the team to play point guard. Tyson Chandler and Brendan Haywood gave the Mavs two more big men to help Nowitzki. Dallas also added All-Star forward Shawn Marion in a trade.

In 2010–11, the Mavericks entered the playoffs stronger than ever before. In the opening round, Dallas defeated the Portland Trailblazers. Next up were the Los Angeles Lakers, who had won the last two NBA titles. The Lakers held a big lead in Game 1, but Dallas fought back to win. The Mavs won the next two games to take command of the series. In Game 4, Dallas connected on one 3-pointer after another. They hit 20 in all to tie an NBA record. The Mavericks won easily, 122–86.

Standing between the Mavs and a return trip to the NBA Finals

were the young and talented Oklahoma City Thunder. For the Mavs to take the next step, they had to control Kevin Durant, the league's scoring leader. The Thunder had an even bigger challenge: controlling Nowitzki. In Game 1, he scored 48 points. Nowitzki went to the foul line 24 times—and made all 24 free throws.

The Thunder tied the series 1–1, but the Mavs captured the last three games. In Game 4, Dallas staged an amazing comeback in the fourth quarter. The Mavericks did the same in Game 5 to close out the series.

Dallas faced a rematch with the Heat in the finals. This time Miami had two new weapons: forwards Chris Bosh and LeBron James. Few outside of Dallas thought the Mavs had a chance, especially after the Heat won Game 1. When Nowitzki injured his left hand, things looked even worse.

The Mavs fell behind in the second half of Game 2, but they refused to give up. Dallas stormed back in the fourth quarter to win on a *clutch* shot by Nowitzki with time running out. The next three games were played in Dallas. The Heat won Game 3 to go ahead 2 games to 1 in the series. The Mavs responded with a victory

in Game 4. Cheered on by their blue-shirted home fans, they held James to just eight points.

Game 5 was another close contest. The Heat led late in the fourth quarter. With Terry struggling, coach Rick Carlisle pulled him out of the game and told him to take a breath and refocus. The pep talk worked. When Terry returned to the action, he played like a *whirlwind*, and the Mavericks won, 112–103.

The Mavs finished off the Heat in Miami in Game 6. Nowitzki exploded for 18 points in the second half, and Dallas played great defense against James from the opening tip-off. The Mavericks also got help from their bench at crucial moments. DeShawn Stevenson and Ian Mahinmi made important shots *down the stretch* for the victory.

When the final buzzer sounded, Nowitzki was named the Most Valuable Player (MVP) of the series. He disappeared under the stands for a moment before coming back out to celebrate with his teammates. After waiting so many years for the NBA championship, Nowitzki needed to have a good cry away from the fans and the television cameras.

LEFT: Dirk Nowitzki dunks over the Thunder in Game 5 of the Western Conference Finals.   **ABOVE**: Mark Cuban leads the celebration from the bench after the Mavs' first NBA championship.

LEADING LIGHTS

Some players lead with their words. Others lead with their actions. The greatest Mavericks inspired their teammates and thrilled Dallas fans by doing both. They are the team's brightest stars.

BRAD DAVIS   6′ 3″ Guard

• BORN: 12/17/1955   • PLAYED FOR TEAM: 1980–81 TO 1991–92

Brad Davis bounced from one team to another before he joined the Mavs in 1980. With Dallas, he became one of the steadiest players in the league. In the spring of 1988, Davis led the Mavs to the Western Conference Finals for the first time.

MARK AGUIRRE   6′ 6″ Forward

• BORN: 12/10/1959   • PLAYED FOR TEAM: 1981–82 TO 1988–89

Mark Aguirre could score from anywhere on the court. The Mavs selected him with the first pick in the 1981 NBA draft. Aguirre averaged 25 points or more for the Mavericks in four different seasons.

ROLANDO BLACKMAN   6′ 6″ Guard

• BORN: 2/26/1959   • PLAYED FOR TEAM: 1981–82 TO 1991–92

Rolando Blackman had one of the best outside shots in basketball. Opponents hated to see the ball in his hands with the clock winding down. Blackman was an All-Star four times with Dallas.

JAY VINCENT   6′ 7″ Forward

• BORN: 6/10/1959

• PLAYED FOR TEAM: 1981–82 TO 1985–86

Jay Vincent had one of the best rookie seasons in Dallas history. He led the team in points, rebounds, and steals. Vincent had the toughness to be a power forward and the quickness to play on the wing.

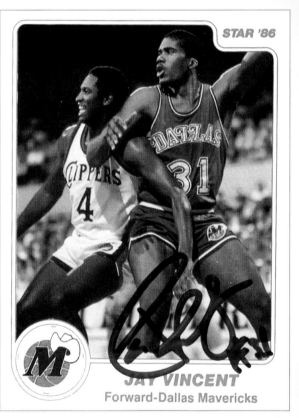

DEREK HARPER   6′ 4″ Guard

• BORN: 10/13/1961

• PLAYED FOR TEAM: 1983–84 TO 1993–94 & 1996–97

Derek Harper teamed with Rolando Blackman to give Dallas a dangerous **backcourt**. Harper was a great shooter and passer. He also made the NBA's **All-Defensive Team** twice.

ABOVE: Jay Vincent

SAM PERKINS   6´ 9″ Forward

- BORN: 6/14/1961   • PLAYED FOR TEAM: 1984–85 TO 1989–90

Sam Perkins used his long arms and athletic ability to make plays all over the court. He played all five positions for the Mavs. Perkins averaged 16 points and 10 rebounds as a rookie.

JAMES DONALDSON   7´ 2″ Center

- BORN: 8/7/1957
- PLAYED FOR TEAM: 1985–86 TO 1991–92

When opponents made it past the Mavs' guards and forwards, they had to deal with James Donaldson. He was one of the NBA's best shot-blockers and rebounders. Donaldson was also one of the league's most *accurate* shooters.

JIM JACKSON   6´ 6″ Guard/Forward

- BORN: 10/14/1970
- PLAYED FOR TEAM: 1992–93 TO 1996–97

Jim Jackson had a "nose" for the basket. When he sensed that he could score, there was no stopping him. Jackson averaged over 25 points a game in 1994–95.

ABOVE: Jim Jackson   **RIGHT**: Michael Finley

JAMAL MASHBURN   6′ 10″ Forward

- BORN: 11/29/1972   • PLAYED FOR TEAM: 1993–94 TO 1996–97

Jamal Mashburn had an amazing combination of strength and *agility*. Unfortunately, an injury cut his career short. But even playing in pain, "Monster Mash" could be a scary player. He was the team's top scorer twice in his first three NBA seasons.

JASON KIDD   6′ 4″ Guard

- BORN: 3/23/1973
- PLAYED FOR TEAM: 1994–95 TO 1996–97 &
  2007–08 TO 2011–12

Jason Kidd began his career with the Mavs. He was co-Rookie of the Year in 1995 and started in the All-Star Game in 1996. Kidd returned to Dallas late in his career and led the team to its first NBA championship.

MICHAEL FINLEY   6′ 7″ Guard/Forward

- BORN: 3/6/1973
- PLAYED FOR TEAM: 1996–97 TO 2004–05

Michael Finley was a great athlete who loved to race up and down the court. The Mavs could count on him for big scoring games and clutch baskets. He averaged more than 20 points a game five times for Dallas.

DIRK NOWITZKI   7´ 0˝ Forward

- BORN: 6/19/1978
- PLAYED FOR TEAM: 1998–99 TO 2018–19

Most fans consider Dirk Nowitzki to be the greatest player in Dallas history. He was as tall as a center and could handle the ball like a point guard. Nowitzki was the NBA's Most Valuable Player in 2007 and the MVP of the 2011 NBA Finals.

JASON TERRY   6´ 2˝ Guard

- BORN: 9/15/1977
- PLAYED FOR TEAM: 2004–05 TO 2011–12

Most NBA players are at their best when they are calm and cool. Jason Terry loved to play with fire in his eyes. On the way to the 2011 NBA title, Terry tied a record with nine 3-pointers in a playoff game.

J.J. BAREA   5´ 10˝ Guard

- BORN: 6/26/1984
- PLAYED FOR TEAM: 2006–07 TO 2010–11 & 2014–15 TO 2019–20

A winning team needs players who can make an instant difference when they get in the game. J.J. Barea was one of the best bench players in the league. During the 2011 NBA Finals against the Miami Heat, Barea was *promoted* to the starting lineup with the Mavs down 2 games to 1. They won the next three games to capture the championship.

SHAWN MARION   6′ 7″ Forward

- BORN: 5/7/1978
- PLAYED FOR TEAM: 2009–10 TO 2013–14

Shawn Marion did not have a weak spot in his game. He used his all-around skill and hustle to make his teammates better. In his second year with the Mavs, Marion helped them win their first NBA championship.

DORIAN FINNEY-SMITH   6′ 7″ Forward

- BORN: 5/4/1993
- PLAYED FOR TEAM: 2016–17 TO 2022–23

No NBA team bothered to draft Dorian Finney-Smith after a fine college career. Slowly but surely, he played his way into the Mavs' starting lineup with great energy and excellent defense.

LUKA DONCIC   6′ 7″ Guard

- BORN: 2/28/1999   • FIRST SEASON WITH TEAM: 2018–19

Luka Doncic arrived in Dallas as a 19-year-old rookie with the skills of a veteran superstar. His shooting, passing, **ball-handling**, and rebounding made him a **triple-double** machine. No one in the NBA is more fun to watch or more feared by defenders.

LEFT: Jason Terry   **ABOVE**: Shawn Marion

X'S AND O'S

For most of their history, the Mavericks believed in hiring experienced coaches who could teach their players how to win. Their first coach was Dick Motta. He had led the Washington Bullets (now the Wizards) to the NBA championship three years earlier. Motta turned the young Mavs into a solid, winning team.

Another coach who made an impact in Dallas was Don Nelson. He came aboard during the 1997–98 season, when the Mavs lost 62 games. In Nelson's third full season, the Mavericks became a 50-win team.

A big change occurred in Dallas in 2000. That year, Mark Cuban bought the team. Cuban ran a successful software company. He wanted the same success for the Mavs. Whatever they needed to win, Cuban gave them. He also became the NBA's most famous fan. Most nights, he could be spotted in the stands, cheering for his team—and letting the referees hear about it when he didn't agree with their calls.

Cuban believed in young coaches who had played in the NBA. In 2005, he promoted assistant coach Avery Johnson to head coach. Johnson had no experience in this position. In fact, he had been a player for the Mavs just two years earlier. But in his first full season, Johnson led the team to the NBA Finals and was named Coach of the Year.

In 2008, Rick Carlisle took over the club. Carlisle had won a championship as a bench player with the Boston Celtics in 1986. He understood how to blend different skills to create a winning formula. In 2010–11, Carlisle led Dallas to its first NBA championship. Carlisle was followed by Jason Kidd. It was Kidd's third time in Dallas, but his first as a coach. He had been part of Carlisle's championship club in 2011. In 2023–24, Kidd led the Mavericks back to the NBA Finals.

LEFT: Dick Motta
ABOVE: Rick Carlisle holds up the championship trophy in 2011.

IN THE MOMENT

DECEMBER 27, 2022

One of the hardest things to do in basketball is to record a triple-double. For a player to finish with double figures in points, rebounds, and assists, he has to play a great all-around game. That being said, not all triple-doubles are the same. Luka Doncic proved that on a December evening in 2022 against the New York Knicks.

The Mavericks treated their fans to an exciting battle that night. The Knicks wanted to prevent Doncic from shooting 3-pointers. They tried to guard him closely when he had the ball far from the basket. Whenever a New York defender got too close, Doncic drove around him and either scored a layup or passed to a teammate. He also made several baskets after setting **screens** and then spinning toward the hoop to receive a pass. This play is called a "pick and roll."

The points kept piling up one after another, but the Knicks found a way to stay in front. They led by nine points with under a minute left. The Mavericks cut the lead to three points with seconds remaining and had the ball. New York fouled Doncic and sent him to the free throw line. The Knicks figured there was no way to make

Luka Doncic splits two New York defenders on his way to the basket—
and a record-setting 60-point game.

three points on two foul shots, right?

Wrong. Doncic thought of a way. After making his first, he missed the second on purpose and the ball ended up back in his hands. He put a shot back up and beat the buzzer. It was good!

The two teams continued their battle in **overtime**. Many fans realized that Doncic already had a triple-double that included 50 points and 20 rebounds. Only two players in history—Wilt Chamberlain and Elgin Baylor—had done this. Now there were three.

At the end of overtime, the Mavericks were the winners by a score of 126–121. Doncic finished with 60 points, 21 rebounds, and 10 assists. It was the first time in NBA history that a player had a triple-double with at least 60 points and 20 rebounds.

WAIT . . . WHAT?

DID YOU KNOW?

The owner of the Mavericks once worked at a *Dairy Queen*. Mark Cuban, who owned the club from 2000 to 2024, not only served ice cream. He worked at DQ while he owned the team! After a game during the 2001–02 season, Cuban was very unhappy with the officials. He joked that the head of the NBA's referees wouldn't even be able to run a Dairy Queen. This gave the people at Dairy Queen an idea. They challenged Cuban to manage one of their stores for a day—and he did! Cuban got behind the counter and served up ice cream to a line of fans that stretched around the block. He learned that waiting on hot, hungry customers was hard work.

ABOVE: When Mark Cuban wasn't scooping ice cream, he was cheering on his team.
RIGHT: This comic book shows James Garner as the "original" Maverick.

DID YOU KNOW?

The Mavericks got their name from a television show. From 1957 to 1962, one of the most popular programs on the air was *Maverick*. James Garner starred as Bret Maverick, a gambler who traveled the Old West with his brother, Bart. Garner was a part-owner of the Mavericks when the team played its first season in 1980–81.

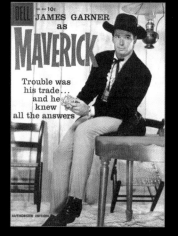

DID YOU KNOW?

The Mavericks had to go to Alaska to find their first star. Brad Davis wore a Dallas uniform for twelve years and was a beloved member of the team. Before he joined the Mavs, he played in Alaska for the Anchorage Northern Knights of the **Continental Basketball Association (CBA)**. Davis had already tried to make it in the NBA, but three different teams cut him. When the Mavs contacted Davis, at first he told them he would rather finish the year in Alaska. Luckily, he changed his mind and joined the team two months into their first season. Davis not only made the starting lineup, he led Dallas in assists six years in a row and set an NBA record for the highest **shooting percentage** by a guard.

UNBELIEVABLE!

Someone must have forgotten to tell Dirk Nowitzki that seven-footers don't compete in long-distance shooting contests. In 2000, Nowitzki entered the NBA's 3-Point Shootout. He finished second. A year later, he came in third.

Nowitzki did not follow the same path to the NBA as other All-Stars. He grew up in Germany, where he learned a different style of basketball. In Europe, every player is expected to be able to dribble, pass, play defense, and shoot. From an early age, Nowitzki showed a special skill for shooting. The taller he grew, the better he shot.

In 2006, Nowitzki entered the Shootout again. This time, it appeared as if he would not make it past the first round. But he made a basket with no time left on the clock to stay alive. By the time the final round began, Nowitzki was on fire. He nailed eight of his first ten shots. The crowd rose to its feet and began to roar. Nowitzki made seven more baskets and took the crown.

When reporters asked if he liked shooting 3-pointers without a defender's hand in his face, he smiled and said, "That's my kind of game!"

Dirk Nowitzki lines up a 3-pointer in 2006. The NBA used special
basketballs for the Shootout.

IT'S ABOUT TIME

The basketball season is played from October through June. That means each season takes place at the end of one year and the beginning of the next. In this timeline, the accomplishments of the Mavericks are shown by season.

1983-84
The Mavs reach the playoffs for the first time.

1999-2000
Hubert Davis leads the NBA in 3-point shooting.

1980-81
The Mavericks join the NBA.

1994-95
Jason Kidd is named co-Rookie of the Year.

2002-03
The Mavs reach the Western Conference Finals for the second time.

Dallas fans bought this souvenir pennant during the team's first season.

Erick Dampier blocks a shot during the 2006 playoffs. He was one of the NBA's best Sixth Men for the Mavs.

2005-06

The Mavs reach the NBA Finals for the first time.

2010-11

The Mavs win their first NBA title.

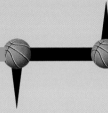

2004-05

Dirk Nowitzki is named First Team **All-NBA**.

2006-07

Dirk Nowitzki is named NBA Most Valuable Player.

2023-24

Luka Doncic is the NBA's top scorer with 33 points per game.

Luka Doncic and Dirk Nowitzki played together for one season before Nowitzki retired.

THAT'S A FACT

MORE MORE MORE

Derek Harper raised his scoring average in each of his first eight seasons with the Mavericks. He was the first player in NBA history to improve eight years in a row.

BUZZER BEATER

In the 2020 playoffs, Luka Doncic hit a last-second 3-pointer to beat the Orlando Magic. At the age of 21, Doncic was the youngest player in history to make a game-winning shot in a playoff game.

KICKING IT

Steve Nash may be a basketball Hall of Famer, but his family's first love has always been soccer. He and his brother Martin—who played soccer for Canada's *national team*—were both first-rate players. After basketball, Nash became an owner of men's and women's soccer teams in the U.S. and Spain.

GERMAN IMPORTS

Dirk Nowitzki was not the first German star for the Mavericks. In 1985–86, Detlef Schrempf and Uwe Blab both suited up for the team.

I'M FLYING

Jason Terry's nickname was "Jet." The three letters in that word are also his three initials. Terry often celebrated baskets by stretching his arms out like airplane wings.

MAN OF THE WORLD

Rolando Blackman was the first player born in Panama to play in the NBA. After his career with the Mavs, he helped coach the Turkish and German national teams.

PASS THE SPINACH, PLEASE

During the mid-1990s, the Mavs' best rebounder was Ron Jones. Jones had a habit of opening one eye much wider than the other and teammates nicknamed him "Popeye" after the famous cartoon character. Jones's sons, Seth and Caleb, became professional hockey players.

LEFT: Luka Doncic   **ABOVE**: Rolando Blackman

37

SPEAKING OF BASKETBALL

"Greatness is not about winning championships, but about the impact you have on others."

▶ **DIRK NOWITZKI,** *on what makes a complete player*

"I have a ***tendency***, especially when I'm playing with great players, to try and get them the ball."

▶ **STEVE NASH,** *on blending in with Dirk Nowitzki and Michael Finley*

"That little J.J. Barea, he was the one who changed the series. We didn't have an answer for him."

▶ **MIAMI HEAT STAR DWYANE WADE,** *on how the Mavs won the 2011 NBA Finals*

"You have to put in the work if you want to see results. There are no shortcuts."

▶ **LUKA DONCIC,** *on the importance of practice*

"Our best player loves passing the ball. It's *contagious*."

▶ **DORIAN FINNEY-SMITH,** *on how superstar Luka Doncic kept his teammates working together*

"To be one of the special ones, you've got to want to take that shot—you've also got to be willing to fail, learn from it, come back and take that shot again."

▶ **JASON TERRY,** *on what makes a clutch shooter*

"When you are surrounded with guys who play at a high level, you don't want to be the odd man out. You want to bring your game up, no matter what age you are."

▶ **JASON KIDD,** *on helping the Mavs win the NBA title in 2011 at age 38*

LEFT: Steve Nash and Dirk Nowitzki chat before a game between the Mavs and Suns. The two stars played together for six seasons in Dallas.
ABOVE: Jason Terry rises for a jumper. He was a fearless shooter.

ROAD TRIP

For fans of the Mavericks, all roads lead to Dallas. But each journey begins somewhere else. Match the pushpins on these maps to the Team Facts, and you will discover the ultimate Mavericks road trip!

TEAM FACTS

1. **DALLAS, TEXAS**—The Mavs have played here since 1980–81.

2. **PITTSBURGH, PENNSYLVANIA**—Mark Cuban was born here.

3. **CHICAGO, ILLINOIS**—Mark Aguirre was born here.

4. **BROOKLYN, NEW YORK**—Sam Perkins was born here.

5. **ELBERTON, GEORGIA**—Derek Harper was born here.

6. **MUSKEGON, MICHIGAN**—Don Nelson was born here.

7. **WINSTON-SALEM, NORTH CAROLINA**—Josh Howard was born here.

8. **SAN FRANCISCO, CALIFORNIA**—Jason Kidd was born here.

9. **HEACHAM, ENGLAND**—James Donaldson was born here.

10. **PANAMA CITY, PANAMA**—Rolando Blackman was born here.

11. **WURZBURG, GERMANY**—Dirk Nowitzki was born here.

12. **LJUBLJANA, SLOVENIA**—Luka Doncic was born here.

13. **MELBOURNE, AUSTRALIA**—Kyrie Irving was born here.

Josh Howard

HONOR ROLL

The great Mavericks teams and players have left their marks on the record books. These are the best of the best!

MAVERICKS ACHIEVEMENTS

ACHIEVEMENT	SEASON
Western Conference Champions	2005–06
Western Conference Champions	2010–11
NBA Champions	2010–11
Western Conference Champions	2023–24

MAVERICKS AWARD WINNERS

ROOKIE OF THE YEAR
Jason Kidd	1994–95*
Luka Doncic	2018–19

NBA FINALS MVP
Dirk Nowitzki	2010–11

COACH OF THE YEAR
Avery Johnson	2005–06

SIXTH MAN AWARD
Roy Tarpley	1987–88
Antawn Jamison	2003–04
Jason Terry	2008–09

NBA MVP
Dirk Nowitzki	2006–07

Shared award with another player.

ABOVE: Jerry Stackhouse starred for the 2006 conference champions.
RIGHT: Dirk Nowitzki clutches his Finals MVP award, while Jason Kidd and Jason Terry raise the 2011 championship trophy.

LEFT: Dirk Nowitzki signed this photo showing his 2007 NBA MVP award.
RIGHT: Avery Johnson and Jason Terry discuss their next move.

Fans bought this pennant after the Mavs' 2011 NBA title.

NOTHING BUT NET

When a Maverick takes aim at the basket, fans hope he hits nothing but net. That is one way of describing a perfect shot in basketball. It does not touch the backboard or the rim and makes a swishing sound that is music to a player's ears. In the NBA, defense is important, but scoring is the name of the game.

The team's first great scorer was Mark Aguirre. He was too quick to be guarded by a forward and too big and strong to be stopped by a guard. In 1983–84, Aguirre set a team record with 2,330 points. That season, he made the most shots in the NBA and finished second in the league with a 29.5 scoring average. The first-place finisher was Adrian Dantley. In 1989, the two stars were traded for each other!

In 2023–24, Luka Doncic passed Aguirre for the team record when he finished the year with 2,370 points. He also led the NBA in points that season. Seventy-three of those points came in one amazing January game, against the Atlanta Hawks. Doncic made 25 of 33 shots—including eight 3-pointers—and 15 of 16 free throws. He broke his own team record of 60 points, set the season before.

Dirk Nowitzki had owned the Mavs' record of 53 points for many years.

Nowitzki's club mark for points in a playoff game might be harder to beat. In Game 5 of the 2006 Western Conference Finals, Nowitzki scored 50 in a victory over the Phoenix Suns. He nearly equaled that mark in 2011, when he scored 48 points in a playoff game against the Oklahoma City Thunder.

Mark Aguirre goes right at Hall of Famer Kareem Abdul-Jabbar. Aguirre's team record for points held up for 40 seasons.

GLOSSARY

BASKETBALL WORDS

ALL-DEFENSIVE TEAM—An annual list of the league's best defensive players.

ALL-NBA—An annual list of the league's best players at each position.

ALL-STAR—A player recognized as being among the best in the league, who is chosen for the annual NBA All-Star Game.

AMERICAN BASKETBALL ASSOCIATION (ABA)—A professional league that played from 1967–68 to 1975–76. Four ABA teams joined the NBA for the 1976–77 season.

BACKCOURT—A term for a team's guards.

BALL-HANDLING—Dribbling and passing skills.

CONTINENTAL BASKETBALL ASSOCIATION (CBA)—A minor league that played from 1970 to 2001.

DRAFT—A yearly event where teams pick from the best college and overseas players.

MIDWEST DIVISION—A group of teams located in the midsection of the country. The Midwest Division was part of the Western Conference for 34 seasons.

NATIONAL BASKETBALL ASSOCIATION (NBA)—A professional league that began in 1946 as the Basketball Association of America and changed its name after merging with the National Basketball League in 1949.

NBA FINALS—The championship series of professional basketball.

OVERTIME—The five-minute period played after a game is tied.

PLAYOFFS—The games played after the regular season that lead to the championship finals.

POSTSEASON—The games played after the regular season, including the playoffs and NBA Finals.

ROOKIES—Players in their first professional season.

SCREENS—Plays where one teammate gets in the way of the player guarding another teammate—without fouling the defensive player.

SHOOTING PERCENTAGE—A statistic that measures how often a player's shots become baskets. Also called field goal percentage. A shooting percentage over 50% (.500) is considered to be very good.

TRIPLE-DOUBLE—A game in which a player reaches double-figures in three categories, including points, rebounds, assists, steals, or blocked shots.

WESTERN CONFERENCE—A group of teams that play in the western half of the country. The winner of the Western Conference plays the winner of the Eastern Conference in the NBA Finals.

VOCABULARY WORDS

ACCURATE—Successful in reaching a target.

AGILITY—The ability to move quickly and gracefully.

ASTONISHING—Extremely surprising.

CLUTCH—Good under pressure.

CONTAGIOUS—Spread through close contact.

DAIRY QUEEN—A business known for its ice cream and milkshakes.

DOWN THE STRETCH—In the final moments. The term comes from the area in front of the finish line in horse racing.

LOGO—A design or symbol used by a business.

NATIONAL TEAM—A group of athletes picked to play for their country in a sport.

OFF-LIMITS—Unavailable or not allowed.

PROFESSIONAL (PRO)—Done as a paying job.

PROMOTED—Given a job with more responsibility.

SOFTWARE—The coded instructions needed to make computers operate.

STROKE OF GENIUS—A sudden understanding of a complicated problem.

SURGED—Increased suddenly.

TENDENCY—A likelihood to behave in a certain way.

UNSELFISH—Willing to share.

VETERANS—People with a lot of experience.

WHIRLWIND—A swirling gust of air that looks like a small tornado.

ABOUT THE AUTHOR

MARK STEWART has written more than 50 books for kids on pro and college basketball. He grew up in New York City rooting for the Knicks and Nets, and held his own in pick-up games in some of the city's toughest playgrounds. He played basketball well into 30s and finally quit when he could no longer dunk. Mark comes from a publishing family. His parents edited and wrote for national magazines and his grandfather was Sunday Editor of *The New York Times*. After graduating with a degree in history from Duke University, Mark wrote for sports and lifestyle magazines and published his first book in 1992. Since then, he has profiled more than 1,000 athletes, many of whom were Mavericks—including Mark Aguirre, Michael Finley, Josh Howard, Kyrie Irving, Popeye Jones, Steve Nash, Dirk Nowitzki, Sam Perkins, Peja Stojakovic, and Jason Terry. Mark wrote the book *Kidd Rocks*, a biography of Jason Kidd, and worked with Kidd and teammate Vince Carter on a photo shoot for *MAR* magazine.

ON THE ROAD

DALLAS MAVERICKS
1330 North Stemmons Freeway
Dallas, TX 75207

NAISMITH BASKETBALL HALL OF FAME
1000 Hall of Fame Avenue
Springfield, Massachusetts 01105

ON THE BOOKSHELF

To learn more about the sport of basketball, look for these books at your library or bookstore:

- Berglund, Bruce. *Basketball GOATs: The Greatest Athletes of All Time*. North Mankato, MN: Capstone Press, 2021.

- Flynn, Brendan. *The Genius Kid's Guide to Pro Basketball*. Mendota Heights, MN: North Star Editions, 2022.

- Peel, Dan. *NBA Legends: Discover Basketball's All-time Greats*. Chicago, IL: Sona Books, 2021.

INDEX

PAGE NUMBERS IN **BOLD** REFER TO ILLUSTRATIONS.

TEAM SPIRIT®

SMART BOOKS FOR YOUNG FANS

The updated, revised, and redesigned **TEAM SPIRIT** series takes the passion for sports to a whole new level. Each book explores the history and culture of a team, and celebrates the timeless connection between the players on the court and the people who cheer them on. New content pulls young readers into age-old debates, while images of classic souvenirs and memorabilia enable them to share the experience of fans from the past.

Every **TEAM SPIRIT** title includes the history of a team, its greatest moments and players, fun quotes, amazing stories, and much more. Each book features a table of contents, index, glossary, timeline, map, and list of sources for further learning.

THE DALLAS MAVERICKS

Children's non-fiction author Mark Stewart brings the spirit and tradition of the Dallas Mavericks to life for young fans. Many of the artifacts and collectibles pictured in this book are from his own collection!

Read all the books in the series to learn more about professional sports. For a complete listing of the teams in the **TEAM SPIRIT** series, visit our website at:

WWW.NORWOODHOUSEPRESS.COM

NORWOOD HOUSE PRESS

ISBN: 9781684500789

9 781684 500789

EVERYDAY
CHINESE MEDICINE

Healing Remedies for Immunity, Vitality & Optimal Health

MINDI K. COUNTS, MA, LAc

PHOTOGRAPHS BY KRISTEN HATGI SINK